BUSINESS

BY

DESIGN

BY

Teresa Elizabeth Bobbe
Amber Schumacher
Jamie Vallejo

Dear Reader,

Here's some truth.

Starting and growing a business is rewarding.

It has a lot of perks (that I am sure you are aware of). But here's some more truth...

Growing a business can be hard. It is not for the faint at heart. There are wonderful moments and some not so wonderful moments and sometimes there are just...well...moments.

Take it from one small business owner to another: starting a business from the roots takes patience, tenacity, grit, knowledge, innovation, creativity, passion, and flexibility, just to list a few.

The authors in this book have all these characteristics and more. As you read their stories, their experiences, and even their steps and tips to help you achieve greatness in your business, remember, they've been through it all. They once were where you are.

They've experienced moments of uncertainty and fear. They've felt unqualified, ill-prepared and unsupported. They've had to pivot what business looks like time and time again. Even during our current stage of the pandemic in July 2020, they've had to pivot once more. But through it all they've realized that with all their business planning, strategy sessions, market analysis, the growth, the lessons learned and successes were all by design. God didn't bring them to anything that He wasn't going to see them through.

He who began a good work in you

Will be faithful to complete it

He who started the work

Will be faithful to complete it in you

(Derived from Philippians 1:6 NIV)

We entitled the book *"Business By Design"* because we; the authors, myself and the publishing staff included, firmly believe that God specially created us individually for our particular businesses and positions. We know our businesses were created by design, and that is what keeps us going during the tough times.

So as you read this book and all yourself to have dreams of your continued growth and success, remember that you were designed for such a time as this and your business can and will flourish - all by design.

Wishing you nothing but growth and success,

Dr. Nicole Long , Publisher and Compiler

Table of Contents

PASSION

AND

SPIRIT

TERESA ELIZABETH BOBBE

It all started when I was a little girl.

I would dream of carnival setups in my backyard and kids coming to the booths with tickets to play games. Small roller coaster rides made from anything I could find in my parents' garage. I advertised and gathered all the neighborhood kids to come to buy tickets and go through the carnival.

I also had a passion for musicals and dancing & set design. I would gather the entire neighborhood and cast each character and rehearse The Musical "Grease" over and over while creating sets and costumes and directing it all. And of course, I had to be Sandra Dee!!

These dreams continued to replay in my mind over and over again with so much clarity. Sometimes it was so clear - I knew one day it had to be my reality.

That's where it all began...

As I got older, I was always creative. I remember watching TV or movies, even the MTV music awards, which honestly, was rare because I was never into TV. I would rather run around and listen to music or go outside. Yet, when I did watch TV, I watched the background. I watched the sets, placement of things, the colors, the brands, etc. I was watching to see how everything was placed together. I was always keen to know more of the transitions, the sets, and the construction of how it all comes together.

So when it was time to think of what I wanted to do with my life and college, you would've thought I already had it figured out. But honestly, I didn't. I was good at school - amazing and intellectually. I was even gifted with a photographic memory... I would skim through my textbooks and pass a test without studying, but I knew the traditional route wasn't for me. On a different spectrum, I dabbled in musical theatre and choir, but that didn't stick either.

One day my sister said... "Hey, this school came and talked to my class today. I think you should check it out". Well, that was that.

I was an artist.

I called FIDM (The Fashion Institute of Design & Merchandising), I applied; I got accepted after several visual projects, tests, and letters. I started in Nov 2004. I set my heart on becoming a Set Designer for Television/Movies. At FIDM, I studied Visual Communications and Interior Design. I worked as a Visual Merchandiser for Bed Bath and Beyond in Woodland Hills. I staged several million-dollar homes while working for a home staging firm in Culver City; it was then when I decided I wanted to start my own Interior Design business. I did that for a while, but I got lost in the party scene, and that was that. I ended up going back to serving at high-end hotels and making a wonderful living on tips.

Fast forward to 2018.

I needed a change. I realized that I was missing out on my passion, and I knew exactly what it was. I knew that Visual Communications and Styling/Set Design were my passion. I knew that the initial dream that I had as a little girl, bringing events to life and sets, wasn't for nothing. I knew even after working in interior designing for corporate that there was more for me to do. I was no longer comfortable dreaming of my dream; my heart was ready to live my dream; I was ready and prepared to live my dream.

So I launched *Free Spirit Productions*.

I am free-spirited, so the name of my business fits me perfectly. I am free, living in my passion, being who I am. Styling, creating visuals, this is what makes me thrive and makes me happy! I was blessed with an amazing eye, an eye to see the design before it's even conceived, an eye to sense and see where things need to be and what colors and what shapes, and whether or not it's symmetrical or asymmetrical.

I was born to make spaces, atmospheres, photos, stages to look and feel just right. So here I am today, pursuing my dream and building *Free Spirit Productions*. One of my niches has to do with building floral to help open up the "necessity" portion of events. In most cases, when someone books an event, they don't think of hiring a designer; they think of the food, the cake, the venue, and the flowers. Well, hiring a designer is much more of a luxury. A luxury that many businesses and individuals alike realized they want for their events. So while in the middle of building my website and growing my clientele and booking, Life happened.

Anyone heard of the coronavirus?!

Boom! Just like that, everything came to a paralyzing halt.

As we compile this book in April 2020, life as we knew it came to a standstill. If you are reading this book in the future, look up the pandemic of 2020, and you will see for yourself.

Now back to the present tense. Here I was trying to get my business off the ground, growing in clientele, and getting my brand out to now only feel like I'm back at square one.

I ask myself, what do I do?

· Do I figure out an idea to keep booking some type of virtual party?

· Do I go through the logistics and brainstorming process of how do all I do virtually?

· Do I allow my ingeniousness to come up with a way to do this entire design process virtually as an actual service and DIY feature?

· Do I take the chance to implement my "Virtual Event Design" service at the risk of having no one book anything right now?

· Do I give up on this dream?

· Do I pivot?

· Do I rest?

What do I do?

All these questions start to flow through my mind, and while I may not have all the answers right now, I know this. As a country right now, we are more open to virtual experiences, and maybe that's here to stay. And I can be a part of that through my online store that acts as an extension to my event styling businesses.

During these very unsettling and very uncertain times, I'm not going to give up; I'm going to pivot. So, I've decided to try and just enjoy the time off with my kids. And even when my mind begins to wonder about the future, I keep telling myself that I'm not alone and that I must realize most of the world is quarantining with me, but I have to have another answer and a backup plan. Like I always say, the average millionaire has 6 streams of income. I can't stress that enough right now! If you own a restaurant, which my parents did for 15 years, I can't even imagine the horror my parents would be going through with nothing else to fall back on. So I think having different avenues of income is a fantastic idea, and that is where my head is at right now, especially during these times where our country is on lockdown.

As I am making peace with that thought - the thought to go ahead and work on the expansion of my online presence and store for my business, another awakening happens. And it's deep.

The awakening for me is about the return of Jesus and the end times. I believe now more than ever that everything is setting a place for the antichrist to come in, and the rapture of the church is coming in our day!

This makes me fearful of the unknown, excited to meet our Lord and Savior, and even sadder to think I may not get to raise my kids and make lots of memories... but it gets me excited all at the same time!

Now you can agree, disagree, or even not care about this, but whatever side of the coin that you are on, it still leaves us questioning our future. Maybe you are a business owner as well, and wondering what is going on during these next days, months for your small business. Or maybe you thought about branching out and starting something of your own and life happenstance. Corona 19, a death in the family, financial uncertainty, has shown up in your life and its making you question everything. Things in life will happen. Tragedy and times of uncertainty are something life promises, but when it occurs, does this mean stop everything and do nothing? No! That is not what God wants any of us to do during these times. He wants us to TRUST His plan! Share with your friends and family, His promises, share even with strangers and be in complete fellowship with Him! Use the purpose He has created in you, the talents He has gifted you with the enhancement and advance of the nation. Spread His love, open up that gift of business, influence new people and live your life free!

So to bring it all home. My goal through these very uncertain times is to

#1 keep my eyes on Jesus!

#2 enjoy every moment with my family and cherish every second because we are not guaranteed tomorrow

#3 focus on new creative ways to build using the gifts that God has instilled in me.

And I challenge you to do the same!

Remember, above all else.

NEVER EVER GIVE UP ON A PASSION OR A DREAM THAT SPARKS THAT INNER FIRE WITHIN YOU! IT IS YOUR CALLING♥ AND ALWAYS KEEP ON PLAYING THE GAME!

GOD HAS GOT YOU!!

XOXO,

TERESA ELIZABETH BOBBE

Free Spirit Productions

Event Design & Floral

"We bring any space to LIFE."

HAPHAZARD LAUNCH

*The Misadventures of An Accidental
Serial Entrepreneur*

AMBER SCHUMACHER

I always say that my journey into business was an accident! That seems to be a recurring theme in my life. I am also an accidental homeschool mom. That's a whole other story in and of itself. Be sure to ask me sometime how that happened. Anyway... when I married my husband, he was already the owner of a thriving construction business. I never really had any desire to have a business of my own or even the desire to help with his. I was still making my way through college toward my Social Science Degree with the assumption that after raising babies, I would go to work in the school district or some area of social work. I did eventually get my degree during my pregnancy with my second son. In my exit interview, when I was asked what my plans were, I answered with, "I plan to be a really smart stay at home mom." My advisor laughed and said, "well, I think that sounds great, and I am not sure I have ever had such an honest answer before." I had found my passion for that season, and I knew for a large chunk of time I was going to be raising kids full time and helping my husband here and there with his business.

A few months after my first son was born, I suffered what I call a major identity crisis. Have you ever suffered from an identity crisis? I sometimes wonder if 'it's a rite of passage for us so we can experience a deeper understanding of being found. Motherhood felt isolating, and I was struggling with an acid reflux baby that never slept. I fell prey to the belief that I needed to prove I could be the perfect mom and wife. I refused to let people see the real me or admit that I was suffering and needed help. I met Jesus at 21 years old, and the transformation in my life was wildly apparent, but motherhood forced me to really face who God says I am. My amazing friend Gina introduced me to a local MOPS's chapter to help me connect with other moms and to get some much-needed refreshing. I spent a year there growing and meeting women in the community. This is the season where my identity began to unfold from head knowledge to heart knowledge. We can know what God's word says and never truly walk in those truths. I had always struggled to have real meaningful relationships with women, so this "mom's group" was super uncomfortable to step into initially. **Funny how God leads us to the end of ourselves to the point where our desperation for Him outweighs what is comfortable.** In this season, God was doing something new in me. He was stripping away lies that I believed about myself and women in general, one layer at a time. Two years later, I had a fire and a passion to serve women that made little sense. Around that time, God opened a door in my home church to start something new for women with young kids. For over eight years, I had the luxury of building a ministry to serve Moms in that church. I was serving almost full time in ministry, leading an amazing team of women for what became a large mom's group in our church. I got a very messy hands-on training while serving women in this capacity. I was young, raising kids, and trying to be a good wife. I literally just jumped right into the deep end. I learned how to build something meaningful with people I loved and cared about. It wasn't always sunshine and daisies, but we grew a ton as individuals and in our relationships. I made a lot of mistakes, but I had amazing women around me to pick me up, brush me off, and send me back into the ring! I learned how to use digital design software, how to plan and budget for ministry (from curriculum to events.) I learned to listen with intention, to observe and ask God to help me see beyond the obvious, to write mini curriculum, to host meaningful and impactful retreats, and to speak from a platform all while learning how to be in real and honest relationships with women. God continued to humble me and reveal new depths of relationship and the value of fighting for people rather than against people. It was an incredible experience that led to me finding a greater purpose than myself. In short, it led to me discovering that God had plans for me to do things that scared me to death and that I never imagined I could do. He is working in me and through me to accomplish His will and purposes. I discovered who I was and that it is fixed; never to be undone. "For *I* am God's masterpiece. He has created *me* anew in Christ Jesus, so *I* can do the good things he planned for *me* long ago." (Ephesians 2:10, emphasis and personalization mine) With that came confidence I had never known before and a passion that has yet to fade to offer encouragement and hope to women everywhere I go. In the still quiet places, with or without a platform.

I loved the ministry that God had entrusted to me. It has become a massive part of who I am today, and I feel the most alive when I am leading and equipping women as they discover their potential and step into their purpose. The ministry was growing, but God was telling me this was going to be a season of intense work. I would shift into raising up the women around me and handing over more and more of my role. At first, it bummed me out. I didn't want to remove myself from the fun and joy that came with being with these women who had become like family. I loved what I was doing, watching women pursue God and people, bravely stepping into their purpose. If I am honest, I struggled to release some control, maybe even my title. I remembered what one of my mentors had told me early on. She told me that, "Our job as effective leaders is to give away so much of ourselves and what God has shown us, that we work ourselves right out of our positions." God had proven to me it was better to be obedient than it was to be comfortable, so I started teaching and training with greater intentionality, intensity, and urgency I had never felt before. What has God proven to you that you can't let go of now? Hold on to that! It will be the catalyst that pushes you beyond where you believe you can go. To my surprise, the relationships God wanted me to focus on took on a whole new depth. In 2015 we discovered that our middle son had special needs. I had that gut feeling for quite some time, but the reality when it was said out loud and put on paper hit me two ways. The first was this rush of relief because now I knew I wasn't crazy. What we were experiencing at home was not typical or a reflection of my parenting or something I could change with a new habit or routine. The other was an utter heartache facing this new reality. We would be challenged with more doctors' appointments, labels, therapy... and we would have to face the misconceptions we had regarding the limited knowledge we possessed in this arena. God would use our questions and our discomfort to move us into a deeper relationship with Him yet again. He was writing pieces of our story that other people would need to hear someday; HOPE.

What seemed like a blink later, we haphazardly launched our third business, but this time it was different.

As we wrestled with the tension of this new diagnosis for our son, my husband was in the middle of a massive battle of his heart and mind. It was an intense season for our family, and I clung to the truths I found in God's word like our lives depended on it. More desperation. More discomfort. **It was a chore to simply breathe sometimes**. Looking back, I can see God had been guiding us and growing relationships around us for this very season. I love how God uses the slow and steady unseen work of growing in our lives. It can be so subtle that we don't even realize it's happening until the fruit is obvious. He had placed people in our lives that had gone before us and could speak life and hope over us. People who showed up without us asking. People who literally carried us, occasionally drug me out of bed, off the floor, out of the house, and prayed with us, for us, over us when we just couldn't seem to find the words or take the next step. God refused to leave me where I was. I can only claim that God was calling me to Him, because it would have been easy to isolate and hide. I had this hunger to dig for a hope I knew was there even when I didn't feel it. I literally combed through scripture every single day looking for truth, hope, grace, courage. I was creating posters with scripture and plastering them throughout our house. I must have looked slightly nuts for a little while. I hammered words of truth into metal washers and keys that I would wear as jewelry. I tucked prayers under my kids pillows. I put scripture above our doorposts and at the entrance of our kid's bedrooms. I wrote God's word up and down my arms. It was a way of meditating on God's word and allowing it to saturate my mind and spirit. Desperate times call for desperate measures. I finally began to speak out about what was going on. Baby steps. A little here, a little there, until the day came that God asked me to be brave and share this piece of my story.

This time around in business, I would have much more involvement than I ever had before, and God would ask me to pour in many of the things He had been teaching me in the ministry world and our life into this business. Transparency and vulnerability were things that made me very uncomfortable. You too? It was scary to consider sharing my life with people beyond my safe little bubble. I mean, this wasn't just about me anymore; it was my husband and my kids. I wanted to protect them and shelter them from the world's peering eyes. There is something miraculous tucked beneath the surface of every one of us. We each have a story, and I believe we were given those stories for a purpose. Once again, I found myself desperate for Jesus. More discomfort. God was asking me to tell MY story. It seemed like terrible timing. My husband was having an incredible crisis of faith. It was our best year in business ever. But he was drowning in a sea of despair. We had been praying for relief for what felt like forever. One afternoon, my husband walked into a job site, and God's word was literally written on the framing of what would become the walls. In the most ordinary moment, God met my husband right where he was in the middle of his mess. I did not understand what our prayers would ultimately bring, but I knew God wanted to answer our prayers. Sometimes the answers to prayers are so simple and so ordinary that if we aren't paying attention, we will miss them completely. It was pretty typical for vendors to drop by and leave catalogs or samples at our office, so it wasn't super weird that a catalog for a laser engraving machine landed on his desk. He brought it home, and I thought, "Oh! That looks like a fun toy." I am pretty sure it sat on our book-shelf for months after that. I mean, does God actually answer prayers with catalogs? Sometime later, during date night, we were talking, and the catalog came up in our conversation. Both of us being creatives thought it would make a fun toy. By the end of the conversation, we were dreaming beyond a toy. I had digital design skills, and my husband is a wildly gifted woodworker (also puzzle solver and creator). What if we could combine our talents? Shortly after this, we were dreaming bigger, fasting, praying, and visiting a trade show. We started with this dream of a little tabletop engraver, and by the time we left, I saw visions of big projects like sugar plum fairies dancing in my head. A week later, we were proud new owners of a giant laser that would require days of training and practice to learn to use and a mountain of guides and books to read. This was the beginning of the end of this construction season for my husband and my accidental second introduction into business and a giant faith-filled blind move to Spokane, Washington. Dare to dream impossible dreams! As Mark Batterson would say, "Circle those God-sized dreams in prayer." Invite some key people in your life to circle those dreams with you. Don't be surprised if He answers those prayers in ways you would never have expected. It took God two years to answer our prayers, and we are still just somewhere in the middle of that answer.

We dreamt of ways to take my heart and passion for ministry and our creative talents to create products that people could take into every space of everyday life. We wanted people to be able to take God's word and encouragement into the most ordinary parts of their day. We wanted others to have hope encounters wherever they were, just like my husband had experienced and just like I had created in our home. We started by just making gifts for friends, family and my ministry. We knew this wasn't the best business plan (I highly recommend having one of those!) We were passionate about what it could be, so we sprinted forward. We started with small projects, and we were pumping out "plaques" faster than they were selling them on our Etsy platform. In hindsight, when was the last time you saw a plaque? Yep, we picked the most dated product ever, and we bought a ton of supplies that we never used up. We probably gave away more than we ever sold. I think we just assumed this would take off as the other businesses did, and we wouldn't need to plan or research e-commerce or trends; I mean, we were practically masters of Etsy with our other business. We jumped into adding custom engraved leather bracelets, and they did great for a while. Until they didn't. So, we would jump to the next product and the next until we found some success with journals, then drinkware and then cheese boards, cutting boards and other kitchenware, and ultimately 3d layered signs. Honestly, if we could engrave hope and encouragement on it, we were doing it. I got to add devotions to the product releases on social media and our blog. It became the ministry I was called to during an interim period of obscurity while God worked on my heart after our big move. **It was quiet work but tucked in it were stories of people that were finding encouragement and hope through our little pocket in the world.**

We never initially defined success by money in this business, but at some point, money matters. We hit some really tough spots our second-year in. As soon as that mindset shifted and money became the gauge in which we defined success, we felt like we were failing, and discouragement set in. We had stopped looking at the original purpose and started leaning into this new definition we were using to define our motives. It wasn't a fair shift in our mindsets, and it set us up with a lot of tension and even some disdain for our business. We really had to go back and remember what we started this all for. Ministry. Our goal was to offer products that encouraged people and gave us a platform to share Jesus. **So, our success here was never meant to be defined by finances.** I think to stay true to your initial purpose and keeping your eyes on your own work is so integral to keeping you accountable to the mission and heartbeat of your business. Has discouragement snuck up on you before? Discouragement is sneaky, it starts with that one not so great review, the plateaued following, or when the numbers are suddenly off with the recent algorithm changes. In a blink, you are in a sea full of crummy attitudes and disappointment. Put that mission statement somewhere you can see it and can go back to it often. Go find the root of your discouragement and ask God to help you uproot it. Don't get stuck in defining success according to someone else's standards, mission, or numbers. Remember the pocket of influence God called you to is on purpose and for a purpose. What is your business' purpose, and are you still aligned with the mission you set out on?

As I write this, COVID-19 has literally brought the world to a screeching halt. I knew back in December 2019 that God would be bringing changes to my business soon. If we expect growth, we must accept change. I kind of drug my feet, shifting into the changes I knew I needed to make. There was not a ton of clarity and was feeling stuck with a lot of things going on in our lives. Dare I say, I felt stuck evaluating WHO I AM once again.

I had been making small incremental steps toward whatever this new thing would be, but I was still holding on to a lot of this business. Perhaps it's because of this faithful and loyal character trait I have. I can sometimes hold on too tight to things that God is asking me to step out of to make room for what is to come. COVID-19 events have forced me to make drastic changes to this business, and ultimately it will look like us closing the engraving side of what we do. I am not afraid though. I am filled with hope and anticipation of what God has planned for the future. I love that He prepared my heart all those months earlier. The original vision and purpose of this business was to offer hope and encouragement, and I know without a shadow of a doubt, that part won't change.

For years now, I have wanted to play it safe and hide behind a computer screen, just writing, posting pictures, and offering great products to encourage people. I was never called to play this life *safe* though. I was not rescued by Jesus and given new life to keep it all to myself and pursue comfort. Somewhere in the process of building this business and moving out of state away from comfort, I grew complacent and let myself make excuses not to show up fully in some areas of my life; one being relationships through the business. I think God allowed me that season to help me see some things more clearly. To teach me things I couldn't learn any other way. God does miraculous work in our season's obscurity. I had let myself buy into the lie that I was supposed to do this alone and not let anyone in. I fell prey to the belief that I didn't have the skills, the experience, or the training to do something valuable. It was my business. I should be able to figure out how to do it all. The product design, the marketing, the media, the management and customer service, the shows, the website etc... I had waited too long to ask for help, and I wasn't clear in which ways I needed it. One day on the long run, I was talking with God about this business and how it was "floundering." He showed up like he always does on the long run for me and hit me with some pretty pointed questions. He asked me what I thought I was doing spending so much time behind the scenes, which is funny because today I am literally stuck behind this screen! He had shown me so many beautiful things about being in relationships with people, and I was hiding on my mountain trying to do relationships in my pajamas in front of my computer screen (without ZOOM and video messaging.) I missed the whole networking and supporting my community piece of the puzzle. Now here is the deal, I love technology and all it has to offer. However, it can never replace genuine, real, tangible relationships. I can see how I veered off track, and today, I am on a mission to go back to the relational part of this mission that always needed to be there. It will look nothing like I can dream up on my own. We all are on a whole new playing field as a nation and world. How will we bridge the virtual world and the physical? God only knows. What I do know is that He is not surprised. Desperation and discomfort will rocket us into a whole new future.

What does that process look like?

These are questions I need to ask myself and God.

1. Who is supposed to be on my team?

There are people that want to invest their time and money into what I have to offer. I don't know why that has been so hard for me to accept. I think I believed in what I created, but not in myself. Where do you struggle to believe that you are worth investing or believing in? You have something to offer. I have something to offer, and I do not need validation from the world or people to get up and go do it. I need to let down my guard; set aside my pride so that I can intentionally pursue people. Have you ever prayed that God would do something for you and then sat around waiting for Him to do the heavy lifting? God requires that we carry out our part. Each of us will be invited to carry out a different part of the story He writes. It isn't up to us to do His part or that of those around us.

When we talk about building genuine relationships, we have to talk about transparency and vulnerability. Not the superficial versions of these we see plastered all over social media pages. The real deal. Transparency is revealing where you have been. Vulnerability is being fully open about where you are. These two things play a huge role in developing valuable relationships with the people I am called to work with. We get to be honest about what we have experienced and what we are experiencing so that we can each run hard and fast in our lanes. Can I be extra honest here? If you are the smartest one in the room everywhere you go, and you never have real struggles to share, then you aren't being honest with yourself or pursuing growth, you are choosing to be comfortable. Make sure there are people ahead of you and behind you. Jesus paints a beautiful picture of this process where we are learning from each other through empowering one another at every mile marker in our lives. There are gifting and insight that my business or ministry requires that I don't possess. It's so important for us to be honest and aware of our strengths and weaknesses so that we can ask for help where we need it or invite others to be a part of where we believe we are called to go. There are experiences I have had that I am charged with sharing with others, and there are things I need to learn from those that are just ahead of me. We don't "arrive" in any part of our journey until we arrive in the Kingdom of God. When I asked God Who He wanted me to connect with, He gave me a list of names! **Don't be afraid to ask God specific questions. Do listen for His response!** I had no idea what each person on my list would say, but it has been incredible to have the conversations. I discovered that people really do want to be a part of this mission I am on, and they believe in me. They are excited to cheer me on. Who is God asking you to invite into this journey?

2. Who am I supposed to interact within my business?

A huge part of what I do requires that I be present with people not just in a business atmosphere but just in ordinary spaces of life. Relying on computer-generated reports and algorithms to tell me where to go or what to do isn't an accurate depiction. Computers cannot access people's hearts. Technology still can't peel back the layers of people to find what it is that lay just below the surface. I can't know what my next move or project is if I am not in the presence of the women God is asking me to serve and lead. Being present with people isn't always super comfortable for me, but God has been reminding me that I need to be present and eager to listen so that I know where to go or what to do next. Try not to show up with an agenda. I get to practice just showing up and leaving room for God to move. Be ready to go do whatever He shows you, and don't be afraid when it looks and feels bigger than you can handle. Be desperate for Jesus and take comfort in knowing He goes before you and with you. Nothing great ever comes out of comfortable spaces. Where are you being called to show up, observe, and listen?

3. How do I go back to my initial mission and go do that right where I am?

People are craving genuine connections more than ever. We are the most "connected" yet most lonely generation ever. Don't be too prideful to say you stepped outside of your mission. Own it and start making whatever changes you need to get back to that first call; the original mission statement. I get to be a part of that, but I must choose to be brave over comfortable. I get to pursue people rather than comfort. This can be hard for the more introverted gals or the ones that fall somewhere between both camps like I do. Recently, I had the pleasure of sitting in at a conference of women with Tiffany Smiley. She said, "Scary is the new fun." She's right. We get to go scared, but the crazy thing is that on the other end of scared, there is a ton of fun to be had and dare I say, freedom. I want to get there, to that place. Just say yes to the next right step, even if it is backwards today. There is never any harm in getting back to that thing God called you to in the first place.

A season of bold yes's and firm no's.

Knowing what to say "yes" to and what to say "no" to takes careful consideration and prayer. I actually find it pretty amusing that just when I got really good at saying "no" to the small things that didn't move my family or me towards where God was calling us, He throws me for a loop and says 2020 will be a season of growth and saying "yes" to crazy things I would have never considered before. I get to say YES to co-authoring this book, but NO to binge watching Netflix series during the COVID-19 stay home order. I get to say YES to a coaching opportunity instead of buying that new outfit I wanted. I get to say YES to leading teams, but NO to that bible study that looks really fun. I get to say YES to sharing my story in turn for saying NO to serving on another team doing amazing things. You know what though, I am here for it. Owning a business and leading in Ministry has forced me to step way beyond my comfort zone. It has forced me to weigh my YES's and my NO's. My filter is asking if this YES will lead me to where I am going or not. There is no magic method or an easy one-sided answer. Each of us will have to make decisions that require sacrifice, but chances are what you will sacrifice won't be what I will. Try writing down your mission and circle it, and then write down all of the things you are doing now or want to do. Determine which of those things move you toward that call and draw a line from the word to the mission. Then put a line through everything else. Did you find things that might not be productive? I always find some conviction when I take the time to look at where I am invested and spending my time and money.

Friend, if I can encourage you in this one thing, then this experience was worth more than I could dream. Don't put Jesus or yourself in a box. As important as your "WHY" is, it is more important to always remember "WHO" you are. That foundation God has laid out for you in the life and death and the resurrection of Jesus Christ is everything. If you have been stuck with a head level understanding of who you are, I am praying for breakthrough over you. That transition to a heart level knowing with every fiber of your being is confidence and freedom that no one can fully put into words, and no human being or experience can ever offer you. From that place, ask yourself what it is that you are passionate about. Does that passion line up with scripture? What makes you unique? What has God given you to share with the world? Pursue intimacy with Jesus and watch Him reveal the kingdom to you right here on earth. One more note on this...It can be easy to fall into the trap of comparison. Especially when we do not feel secure in who we are. We have all heard the adage that comparison is the thief of joy, but if you ask me, a comparison is the thief of all the things. It quickly robs you of contentment, peace, joy, hope, grace, courage, and so on...it even robs us of a chunk of our identity. Don't ever forget who you are or the unique attributes that set you apart. Keep your eyes on the kingdom, and don't let them wander all over the world. Don't be a peeping tom...Keep your eyes in your own window.

Let others in but be wise as to who you let take up valuable real estate in your heart and your mind. No matter where you are in your business journey, there will be people that are for you and a few who are against you. Maybe you have already encountered those people? Don't take it personally. I have found that most people that seem to be against me are against pieces of me that remind them of their hurts, not me, in general. There are always roots we cannot see just below the surface. Keep a journal of your thoughts and make sure you have a few safe people to turn to when things get rough. John 15:13 says,

"Greater love has no man than this, that a man lay down his life for his friends." I like to call these my 10% friends. They are the people in my life that I trust to tell me the last 10% of the truth that no one else would ever dare to tell me. They are also safe places for me to turn when my thoughts run away with me. You know what I am talking about, the hard truths that we all need to hear or see at some point in our lives. People earn that positioning in your life as you invest in one another through the ups and downs of life. Give permission to those people to speak into your life.

Girl! Don't get stuck waiting for someone to get you to the next spot or point you to do the next right thing. Only you and God can *actually* get you where you are going. Mentors are amazing. Get you some. But don't get stuck waiting for the perfect coach or perfect mentor and never blame someone for where you aren't yet. God will bring you the right resources at the right time. Don't hop into a cycle of waiting for someone to share the next great tool, coaching, or resource. Be a self-learner and pursue wisdom and knowledge. In my opinion, it is better to be doing something and fail than to be doing nothing and never find out what might be waiting for just one brave step in front of you. Romans 8:28 Tells us that, "All things work together for the good of those who love the Lord and are called according to His purpose." Owning a business; being an Entrepreneur is an interesting world, and it is filled with times of fun, wins, and success, along with utter failures and setbacks. **If we threw up our hands with every speed bump, set back, and failed attempt, we would not have the innovation we see all around us today.** I bet if you asked most successful entrepreneurs, you would find that they failed more times than they succeeded but that what they learned in those places is what got them to where they are today. The entire game changes when you know that there is a purpose for your work in you and through you. It is imperative for us to remember all things; good and bad are working together for good to bring about a plan or purpose not set by us. We get to choose to look beyond the obvious to find the lesson or the next move.

Stay humble. Colossians 3:12 commands us, "Therefore, as God's chosen people, holy and dearly loved, clothe yourselves with compassion, kindness, humility, gentleness, and patience." Don't forget who you are or where you come from or those that have influenced your success. I think that the most tangible way we can make sure to keep this heart posture is to elevate those around us over seeking to elevate ourselves. I want to point people to Jesus, not myself. As soon as that shifts, I lose the influence and authority that was entrusted to me.

Every week I get to take stories of my own life and let God show me how to use them to encourage others and point them back to Jesus. Whether that is dropping pieces of that story on a tumbler, the cover of a journal, coaching my team or speaking to women, I get to breathe life over people and help them take hold of hope, encouragement, and joy wherever they go. I am living out that dream prayer I circled, watching God meet people in the middle of their brokenness, their mess, and finding hope in the most unlikely of places through stories and God's word. I pray we would never give up on the dreams God places in our hearts despite every up and every down. Galatians 6:9 reminds us, "So let's not get tired of doing what is good. At just the right time, we will reap a harvest of blessing if we don't give up."

I am rooting for you!

I can't wait to hear and see what God is up to as you pursue bravely stepping into WHO you are and the purpose God placed in you.

A BUSINESS OWNER

OWNER

From

THE INSIDE

OUT

Jamie Vallejo

Back in 2014, I led a finance team in corporate America during the day and was completing my MBA in the evening. It was easy to say that I didn't have a life. Amid this demanding season of life, I heard a voice clearly say to me, "Pack your bags, and let's go on a road trip." I was in the middle of studying for my finals at the end of my last quarter, quickly approaching, and it was also month-end, which was the busiest time for me at work. The timing wasn't perfect, but the voice was ever so clear. I had complete peace about asking for the time off and getting my finals done so early so that I could leave ASAP. With no hesitation, both my boss and professors permitted me. I packed my bags, dropped the top of my convertible, and headed south away from the concrete jungle of city life in Chicago to the serene mountains of Tennessee.

Looking back, I thought I was prepared for this trip, but nothing could prepare me for the change I was about to endure. I had no idea what was about to happen to me. I came back from that trip a WHOLE new person, and I have never been the same since. Let me tell you why:

"The two most important days in your life are the day you were born and the day you find out why." Mark Twain

It was on this trip when I found out "my why."

Here's a little backdrop on my life up until that point. I was raised with an emotionally absent father, though he was present, but only physically. This lack of an emotional relationship had a huge influence on my life that left me hitting rock bottom with horrible abusive relationships with men and a career where I felt trapped. I found myself on my knees in my lonely apartment, going to the one relationship that I knew could help me, yet I stayed distant in the past several years, and that was my relationship with God. I **felt so ugly and unwanted, and I asked God to take over.** I can't do it anymore. I felt a release, and I felt His presence.

Then I asked Him what I asked all my boyfriends, "Am I beautiful?" I asked Him this because I was tormented for decades with the false beliefs about my beauty. I believed I was only as good as I looked on the outside. This lie led me to one bad decision after another, and after each bad decision, I was left living with huge insecurities, and I became a puppet to the circumstances that played out in front of me. It took a decade from the day I was on my knees in my apartment to hear the answer to my question finally. A ten-year journey of deep and self-discovery healing to finally be in a position to hear the answer from God to my question, "Am I beautiful?"

It was in those beautiful Smoky Mountains in Tennessee where He gave me the answer. I didn't realize that when I was asking this question, that I would find my purpose in life because of the answer to this question.

I was enjoying the fresh air in the mountain. I saw the beauty of the grass fields, flowers, the trees, the extraordinary views from the tops of the mountains. I ate delicious food in the mountains. I listened to the beautiful sounds of the birds and nature and felt the lovely warmth from the sun on my face. As I experienced all of this, I felt God place in my heart my answer. He said,

> "You see, Jamie, your beauty is like my beauty, it
> is multidimensional. Just like you enjoy my
> creation from all your senses, your beauty is

magnified when you see it as more than just what's on the surface level. I created your beauty to be multidimensional. Every aspect of you – "your personality, your gifts, your mannerisms, your loud, vivacious laugh, your ability to love and serve others, your dreams, your ability to see me in all aspects of your life, your ability to find the joy I have for you in this life," makes you beautiful. If you want to portray the beauty that reflects me, then look at your beauty from a multidimensional perspective. This is how I see your beauty, and this is how the heavenly Father sees your beauty."

I sat there in the mountains with tears of joy in my eyes. For the very first time, I was looking at my beauty the way God designed it. And I had my answer – I was beautiful.

I knew immediately that **this** definition of beauty was not just for me. God wanted me to share this definition with women all over the world. He wanted His daughters to know how they should see their beauty because I knew for a fact what one believes about their beauty is how they will live their life, and I want to make sure that every woman lived it in a big way.

I read the following excerpt from a book called "Chosen," written by Michelle McClain.

"Anytime you read in the Bible that God is calling His people to a mountain or hill, you know the agenda of heaven is about to invade earth.

As one goes up to a mountain or hill, she is ascending to higher altitudes. She is going up to a place that is on a higher plane than she usually stands on.

So, ascending the mountain of God represents a change in perspective or vantage point. It represents a paradigm shift or awakening. It is an invitation to go higher and think higher. In this place, the dream of God is revealed for the earth. The CHOSEN one postures her HEART to receive the invitation to change her perspective."

It was in the mountain tops of Tennessee where God gave me His dream for the definition of beauty. Multidimensional beauty was downloaded into my heart and ignited a fire of passion inside of me.

I believe that you are no different than me; **I believe God wants to show you His purpose for your life and elevate you to walk fully in your purpose.** If you have not taken the time to go inward and discover your inner beauty, then I want to encourage you to do it now. What time would be a better time to do so? When you are thinking about starting a business? I believe the insight you will gain about yourself will pull you forward in your dream of starting a business.

When I was in my MBA program, I read a book called "Start with Why" by Simon Sinek. This book really moved me, and I felt like I was brought in on the biggest secret to having a successful business. I believe a business is not just about getting a great product to a consumer; there are so many great products out there in the world. I believe wholeheartedly that the best businesses are not businesses; they are movements. Simon shares his discovery of how successful businesses have pulled this off with "The Golden Circle." The best businesses start with why.

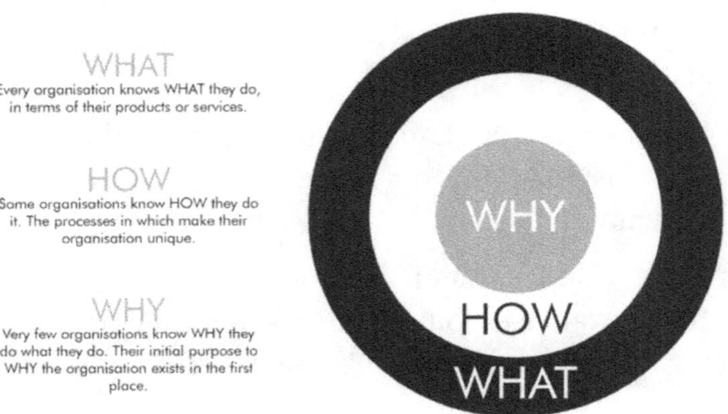

My second recommendation is to read this book, study it, and know your WHY when building your business. I believe when you know your "WHY," it will help the "How and What" come into place.

MAKE MONEY NOT INSTA-FAME

My second bit of advice for anyone who is starting a new business is to focus on making money, not being famous. Now, you might be a little confused, and thinking, didn't you just tell me to start a movement. Don't I need a bunch of followers to start a movement?

Great question. I am glad you asked. Let me tell you the difference between being famous and starting a movement. First off, if you are going into business, you want to make a profit. If you just want to be famous, you don't need to make money to do that on social media. Don't let the high number of followers on anybody's social media accounts fool you. It does not mean that they are making money.

I recently had a meeting with the head of a top PR Agency for social media, who has worked with top accounts on social media. She said there are plenty of accounts she works with that have only a couple of thousands of followers where the business is making millions of dollars and accounts with millions of followers barely bringing in a dollar.

I bring this to your attention because I spent years trying to build a following. I exhausted myself and got so discouraged year after year when I didn't see my following grow. It killed my spirit every time I lost a follower. You don't want to be a puppet to the daily, even hourly increase and decrease of followers. I have a background in finance, so I have been trained for decades to trend the numbers up. I had to look at my bigger vision of the company and determine the best path to my current goals. After taking a step back and looking at the global vision, I realized I had everything I needed to get started—just ten loyal raging fans of the INNER BEAUTY movement. As a Christian and believer of Christ, it was a reminder that Jesus invested deeply in His 12 raging fans, the disciples that created a movement that has touched multiple billions of people in the world.

Now, back to the clarification between building a movement and gaining followers. Be honest with yourself and know why you are doing what you are doing. One of the biggest things I have learned in life is to be successful. You have to be honest with yourself to understand why you do what you do. If you are leading your business with a servant's heart, you are always going to put your client first and do what is best to help them. By thinking of your client and creating content, services, and or products that help them, that will make their life better and help them in achieving their goals, and this is what it's all about. It is very easy to fall prey to wanting to gain followers for the sake of gaining followers. Permit me to say it bluntly, building a following for our own egos. You don't have to worry about having a huge following to give you the confidence that you are an expert at what you do or provide. You are already an expert. Your life up until this point has proven you an expert. If you need a huge following to validate it, then you might as well get ready for a shaky right to entrepreneurship because if your worth is tied into a following and not in who you are on the inside, you will be a puppet to all the difficulties of entrepreneurship. If you are that sensitive, any little negative circumstance that comes your way can quickly shake you. So, build your worth on a solid foundation.

In making money, you want to ensure that you are moving your vision along where making money is the result. If you are not making a profit (Profit = sales revenue - costs of product/service) in exchange for your product or service, then you simply have a hobby. Always make sure that 100% of your daily activities on your business move you towards your profit, especially when you are just starting. Make sure you never put any time and daily working activities of building a following over making a profit. The profit should always get the priority, or you will never get your business off the ground.

BE VISION LED

Another huge lesson and breakthrough for me was being a vision-led leader instead of an operational leader. Let me explain. Operations are essential in a company; however, focusing just on operations kept me stuck for 2-3 years. If you are someone who is currently working in corporate America like I was, listen up. You are programmed as a corporate employee to do lots of project management. If you went to school for a technical skill like I did in finance/accounting, they taught you everything about your one particular industry. You see, there is a difference between creating the finance/accounting industry, and being trained in the industry that has been around since the 1400s. Therefore, as a finance/accountant expert, I was trained on how to do a skill-set that has been mastered for years. You know what it looks like when you are excelling at it, and you know what it looks like if you are not excelling at it. To me, it's pretty black and white, and my whole corporate career was about learning general accounting principles and mastering them.

As an entrepreneur, I can respect governance, policy, and procedures, but when it comes to starting with a new business, it was killing my ability to create. **I never knew I could create, let alone how to create.** As an entrepreneur, you are creative because you are creating a business that has never been done. You might say, well, there are already multiple businesses out there like the one you are about to build. Yes, that is true, but if you mimic your business just like the rest, what will make yours stand out? Of course, we should definitely learn from other business models what works and what doesn't work and implement our learnings into our business, but what I proposed to you earlier, starting a movement versus starting a business is something we should do to stand out and reach the clients we genuinely want to help. Again, this is the secret sauce to a successful and thriving business, and with you in the mix, no one can duplicate it quite the same.

I believe in a higher calling in life, and for that calling to come to pass, I have to look to a higher entity on how this calling for my life will come to pass. I shared with you earlier my calling in life to help women restore the way they see their beauty, and that's the way God designed their beauty specifically for them. **This is my calling.** My business is a lifestyle coaching business. My mission is to create spaces where women can connect with God and download the definition of their beauty into their hearts, similar to my story. It overwhelms me when I think of the bigger vision of a stadium as big as Soldier Field full of women on fire for the definition of Multidimensional beauty, which I believe is the definition of beauty. How will I ever make that happen?

One thing I learned is to be vision-led. In the past, I used to make daily decisions on trusted facts of my industry-based experience and know every day by looking at the numbers if I was getting closer or not. You can't do that when you are vision led. You have to be open to a result that might not look like you would think it should look like. As a result, I found myself hitting walls and being stuck several times because I was so scared to take risks. My training taught me to be educated enough to make decisions that are proven to be successful, so I never thought twice about executing a plan that is uniquely my own. But when you are building a new movement that has never been done before, there is no history, and there are no proven facts. Where this used to frustrate me, it now excites me to know that the plan is totally open! I now love the idea that life is full of so many opportunities, and that creating something new will require innovation – doing something new. This will spark the flame and grow it into a stadium. I learned that life could be fun and not so restricted. I learned that, although governance and policy has its place, yet this is not the perfect space for me to start a movement. It took years before I could let go and learn more about being creative.

For those of you who are like me, starting a business with zero investors and very little money, I want to tell you it is possible to make your dreams of a business come true. The best businesses innovate! And the beauty of your situation is that you have little overhead. The best quality that you need to innovate is to be flexible, to make quick decisions, and move. Big companies and corporations cannot do this. Right now, you don't have any policy and procedures or a huge group of employees that you need to steer in any direction. It's just you.

You might be thinking, but I need resources like people, money, and equipment to get my business off the ground. I understand you. Let me share with you something that took me years to figure out.

You have everything you need to start your business. Here is the formula to make it happen:

Limited Resources + Willingness to Fail + Increasing Passion = Exponential Innovation

I learned this from one of my favorite leaders, Craig Roechel. Limited Resources forces you to go within. Innovation starts from within. The ideas are there, and we just have to focus our energy on the inside.

Right now, as I write this, we are on week 2 of social distancing set in place by the government as COVID-19 is invading the world. I have been on many Zoom calls like most of you with fellow business owners, and the fear of the future is real. I get it. So many small business owners are experiencing a shift, where their current business models are being shut down for the time being. I think now is a time where it's forcing business owners to understand the importance of always being flexible and always working on innovating their business. The best in their industry are paving the way, utilizing innovation to create the future of business as we know it. I believe our current situation is a playground for us to see the opportunities that are sitting right in front of us.

One fact I want to leave you with as we close out this chapter is that the following start-ups were founded in the 2008-2010 recession:

1. Uber

2. Airbnb

3. Slack

4. Pinterest

5. WhatsApp Inc.

6. Square

7. Venmo

I am a firm believer that God is a God of abundance and has a future of hope to help us, prosper us, and not to harm us. I believe we are forced into our current situation to have a perspective. We will look at our situation in fear, which will give us a lack of perspective, or will we look at our situation with faith to discover our abundance perspective.

I believe that now is the time that business owners with an abundance perspective will create the future for most recognizable companies of our time because they will implement their ideas and change the way we do business forever. What perspective do you have for your business? How can your business be one of these businesses?

These are questions we all need to ponder on.

AUTHOR BIOGRAPHIES

TERESA ELIZABETH BOBBE

Author of *Passion and Spirit*

Teresa Elizabeth Bobbe is an EVENT DESIGNER interior designer, set designer, and full-time mom. She has starred in her family's pizza restaurant commercials, starred in a fox family tv show, and graduated from the famous F.I.D.M. She full-time rv lives and travels with her two wonderful and creative children and enjoys living the nomadic life!

If you would like to have her design your special space you may contact her @ Freespiritproduction1@gmail.com or via FB: https://www.facebook.com/freespiriteventstyling/

$\curlyvee$AMBER SCHUMACHER

Author of *Haphazard Launch*

Amber Schumacher loves God sized adventures and she believes that every moment is a personalized invitation to the greatest adventure a person can experience on this side of heaven. She believes in the power of storytelling and deeply rooted relationships. Every story matters and she loves that we get to use them to empower others, offer hope and encourage people to grow. She is passionate about experiencing the extraordinary in the everyday ordinary moments of life. Coaching women as they discover how to jump into passion, potential and purpose is one of her greatest joys next to exploring with her 3 kids and husband of 16 years. She has been writing devotions, creating group curriculum, and speaking to women's ministry groups for over 10 years. A serial entrepreneur, she has built three businesses with her husband and together they are launching their fourth. She is the first to laugh about their mistakes and embrace change ... after a good cry over a trendy cup of coffee of course.

⌒JAMIE VALLEJO

Author of *A Business Owner from The Inside Out*

Jamie Vallejo is a inner-beauty lifestyle coach who supports women in unveiling their own unique beauty and walking boldly in it. She works with an extensive diverse group of women and is gifted with the ability to see her clients unique beauty and helps them to make it the very essence of themselves. Jamie truly comes to life when she sees her clients embracing and magnifying their unique beauty onto others, inspiring others to pursue their own unique beauty. It's the gift that keeps on giving.